the Talking Edge

Co-operActivities in EASY Communication

By MICHELLE BUEHRING

JOAN ASHKENAS, Editor

Illustrations by
SUSAN ENGELMAN BLOCK

JAG PUBLICATIONS

Special Thanks

Special thanks go my perpetually inspiring colleagues Danielle Keesee, Elizabeth LeGlaire and Jack Walker, and my editor, Joan Ashkenas. I am indebted to Robert Austin at the Doheny Eye Bank, Geneva Carney at the American Tort Reform Association, Robin Lossing and William Bloomfield at Citizens Against Lawsuit Abuse, the Loudoun County School District, and Bob Spieldermer at United Network for Organ Sharing. Without their kind e-mail responses, my research would have been considerably more difficult. Lastly, my deepest gratitude to Klaus, Hannah and Alex for giving me the freedom and time to write this book. You guys are everything to me.

© 2000 JAG Publications
co-operActivities® is a registered trademark of JAG Publications

All rights reserved. No part of the publication may be reproduced or transmitted in any form or by any means without the written permission of the publisher.

Published by:
JAG Publications
PMB301
11288 Ventura Boulevard
Studio City, CA 91604

Telephone and fax: 818 505-9002
e-mail address: info@jagpublications-esl.com

Design and production by Jack Lanning

Printed in the U.S.A.

10 9 8 7 6 5 4 3 2 1

Library of Congress number: 99-73750

ISBN 0-943327-23-7

To the Students...

Sometimes it is not easy to speak in a group. Sometimes you don't feel sure about what to say. *The Talking Edge* gives you the chance to talk freely about some important and interesting subjects.

The stories here really make you think. The exercises help you build new vocabulary and they are fun to do. Don't be afraid to say what you think because there are no right or wrong answers.

You will probably need to use the dictionary to look up vocabulary. If you need some extra practice looking up words, the dictionary lesson at the beginning of the textbook is very helpful. You can review it by yourself or with the class. Use it as often as you need. You should also look for meanings of words in the Helpful Vocabulary list after each story. In addition, you will find chapter notes and answers to exercises at the back of the book.

The Talking Edge can help you to be a successful English speaker in your daily life as well as in the classroom. The author wishes you many exciting conversations in the future.

To the Teacher...

Often our ESL students find themselves unable to converse with native speakers because of their lack of knowledge about the subject matter, limited vocabulary, or insecurity about their opinions. How well do we, as teachers, actually prepare our students for the "outside world" of conversation and intelligent discussion? Student success outside the classroom is a goal for which we ESL teachers strive.

The stories in **The Talking Edge** contain much cultural information along with enormous potential for vocabulary-expansion. The controversial topics help students express their thoughts in a non-threatening environment as they realize that their opinions are not seen as right or wrong.

Dictionary Lesson. Students are encouraged to use the dictionary to help expand their vocabulary. Although a **Helpful Vocabulary** list follows each reading, students may still require individual practice using a dictionary. For that reason, a concise, self-paced dictionary lesson appears at the start of the text. You may also review it orally as a class exercise if you prefer.

Co-operActivities. *You will need to check the Chapter Notes and Answer Key for help with the activities.* There are twelve chapters, each of which revolves around one controversial news story. Through classroom discussions, debates, story relays, role-play, word games, interviews and other **Co-operActivities**, students are equipped with the knowledge, vocabulary and confidence they need to discuss issues that affect society today. The **Co-operActivities** in the text almost never repeat. However, most of the them can be interchanged among

To the Teacher...

the chapters. If your students particularly enjoy one, you may adapt and use it for another chapter as well. Choose the **Co-operActivities** your students enjoy and that time allows.

Warm-up. Each chapter begins with a warm-up activity that relates to the story in some way. The **Warm-up** activities are all different. Students are asked to recall an event, rank characteristics, create a story, relay information, send a message or predict an outcome.

Vocabulary. The **Helpful Vocabulary** list appears after each story as a convenience to students. It will enable them to read the story quickly and avoid time usually spent referring to a dictionary. Please be aware that the definitions in the **Helpful Vocabulary** are given only in the context of the story. Also, each word's part of speech has been noted.

Comprehension. Comprehension questions follow each story. They serve to test and reinforce understanding of new vocabulary and story content.

Discussion. The **Discussion** questions allow students to deal directly with content and apply background information and new vocabulary to discuss their opinions.

Answer Key and Notes to the Chapters. Located at the back of the text, this section lists the sources for each story and adds to the facts of the issues presented. It also contains information for using the **Co-operActivities** in the classroom. Answers to the comprehension questions, puzzles, games and story outcomes are found here as well.

TABLE OF CONTENTS

	To the Students…	3
	To the Teacher…	4
	A Dictionary Lesson	8

CHAPTER 1 *An Act of Kindness* — 10

Co-operActivities: A Hospital Memory
Role-play Rotation
Guess the Ending

CHAPTER 2 *English Only — At Work* — 14

Co-operActivities: Deciding MOST to LEAST
Back-to-Back Dictation
Job Role-play

CHAPTER 3 *For Love and Money* — 20

Co-operActivities: Who Got Audrey's Money?
Role-play Interview
Memory Cloze
The Same Face

CHAPTER 4 *Tradition in a New Country* — 26

Co-operActivities: Animal Facts Jeopardy
The $25,000 Vocabulary Game

CHAPTER 5 *Cases of Coffee and Candy* — 32

Co-operActivities: Send the Messenger
In Your Own Words
The Line-up
Skit

CHAPTER 6 *America's First People*   *38*

   Co-operActivities: A picture Says a Thousand Words
                                   Guess the Facts
                                   Pair Reading
                                   The 45–Second Board Game

CHAPTER 7 *A Good Education*   *44*

   Co-operActivities: Story Relay Race
                                   Counting Nouns
                                   Facts of the Story

CHAPTER 8 *A Perfect Copy*   *48*

   Co-operActivities: Introduction Cloze
                                   Story Mix-up
                                   Making Questions

CHAPTER 9 *No Blood!*   *52*

   Co-operActivities: Story Line
                                   Get the Whole Story
                                   Soap Opera
                                   Classroom Feud

CHAPTER 10 *Who Will Donate?*   *58*

   Co-operActivities: Make a Story
                                   Pair Reading
                                   Understanding FOR and AGAINST
                                   Do You Know Your Past Tense?
                                   Vocabulary Mini-Bingo

CHAPTER 11 *Scott's Choice*   *66*

   Co-operActivities: What Happens Next?
                                   Vocabulary Through Pictures
                                   Word Links

CHAPTER 12 *Women Only*   *70*

   Co-operActivities: Timed Reactions
                                   Ask a Teacher

Answer Key and Notes to Chapters   *75*

Learning to Use the Dictionary

I. Alphabetizing

Use the alphabet to help you do the following exercises.

a b c d e f g h i j k l m n o p q r s t u v w x y z

1. Put these letters in correct order:

    b   c   a   _____ _____ _____

    i   g   h   _____ _____ _____

    o   m   n   _____ _____ _____

2. Put these words in correct order according to their first letters:

    sit   baby   light   house   _____ _____ _____ _____

    fast   apple   cake   down   _____ _____ _____ _____

3. These words have the same first letter. Arrange them according to their second letters:

    buy   big   boy   black   _____ _____ _____ _____

    pin   pan   put   pet   _____ _____ _____ _____

    shell   sell   spell   same   _____ _____ _____ _____

4. These words begin with the same two letters. Put them in order according to their third letters:

    plan   plum   plot   _____ _____ _____

    flock   flake   flute   _____ _____ _____

    street   stamp   stop   _____ _____ _____

    through   thought   thin   _____ _____ _____

II. Using the Dictionary

Open the dictionary to where the letter 'b' begins. Notice that the first words you see following the 'b' all have 'a' for their second letter. Now look at their third letter. Notice that these third letters follow in alphabetical order: first 'a', then 'b', then 'c', through the rest of the alphabet. Using this idea, let's practice and look up the following words: baby, back, bad, bag.

Now turn the pages and pass the letters 'ba' until you find words beginning with 'be.' Look up these words: beach, bed, before, begin.

Now continue turning pages until you find words starting with 'bi.' Find these words: bicycle, big, bill, bird.

Now look for these words: black, boat, brake, bud.

III. Dictionary Work

Open the dictionary and look at the top of any page. You can see two words in dark letters. The word on the left gives you the first word on the page. The word on the right gives you the last word on the page, and between these, all words are in alphabetical order, according to their second, third, fourth, etc. letters.

Let's practice finding some words. Turn to the letter 'b' and look for the word 'bad.' You know it is close to the beginning of the 'b' because its second letter is 'a.' It comes after words beginning with 'bab' and 'bac' because 'b' and 'c' come before 'd' in the alphabet.

Let's try another word. Turn to the letter 'n' and find the word 'not.' The second letter, 'o', of 'not' is more towards the middle of the alphabet, so you must pass words beginning with 'na', 'ne', 'ni', and find words beginning with 'no'. Now you need to find the third letter, 't', after the 'o'. Look for it in its alphabetical order at the top of the pages in dark letters.

Using what you know, you can now look up any new words in the dictionary as you read.

CHAPTER 1

An Act of Kindness

Warm-up

Co-operActivity: A Hospital Memory

Draw a simple picture of a time when you or someone you know had to go to the hospital for a medical problem. Then, choose one of the following activities.

    A. Use your picture to explain to your partner what happened.

B. Don't put your name on your drawing. Your teacher will collect all the pictures and give you one that belongs to another student. Explain the picture (as you understand it) to your partner. Then, with your partner, try to find the student who drew it. Ask him or her what really happened.

An Act of Kindness

It is the first week of school. Five-year old Sean Landaverde is very unhappy. He does not want to go to his classroom. His classmates are unkind. They laugh at him and say unfriendly things. He has fights with the other children on the playground.

Sean Landaverde has a problem. He has very, very big ears. Every day someone says something about them. "I'm Dumbo," Sean says. Sean is a healthy and beautiful boy, but he feels that he is "different" from the other children.

Sean's parents want to make him happy. They asked their doctor about an operation to give Sean normal ears. The operation costs $4,000. Insurance companies pay for many operations, but Sean's insurance company said that this kind of operation is unnecessary because it is only a beauty correction. Sean's family does not have enough money to pay for the operation.

Helpful Vocabulary

fight (n.) – argument or action of hurting someone
playground (n.) – play area
insurance company (n.) – company that pays money to take care of you if you have accidents or sickness. You pay the company each year for this.

The Talking Edge

Comprehension

Answer these questions. You may look back at the story for the answers.

1. Why is Sean unhappy the first week of school? _____.

2. Are Sean's classmates nice to him? Explain. _____.

3. What problem does Sean have? _____.

4. The insurance company doesn't want to pay for the operation because _____.

Discussion

Answer these questions with a partner or in a group.

1. Who is your doctor?

2. Do you speak English with your doctor?

3. Do you like the way you look? Why or why not? Do you want to change anything about yourself?

4. Do you agree with the insurance company that Sean's operation is unnecessary? Write your answer here:

_____.

Chapter 1   An Act of Kindness

Co-operActivity: Role-play Rotation

You will become an actor in the story. Some possible actors are: Sean Landaverde, Sean's teacher, Mr. Landaverde, Mrs. Landaverde, Sean's unkind classmate, Sean's kind classmate, the insurance company supervisor.

Next, the class makes a double line, so each actor (each student) sits face-to-face. For example, you are Mrs. Landaverde and you are sitting face to face with the insurance supervisor. What do you want to say to him/her?

You have two minutes to talk to the actor/student facing you. Tell the student what you can or can't do for Sean's problem. After two minutes, you will move to the next seat. Now you have a different actor to talk to for two minutes. (Sometimes you may be face-to-face with your same actor.) Continue to the next actor every two minutes until you speak to everyone in the story.

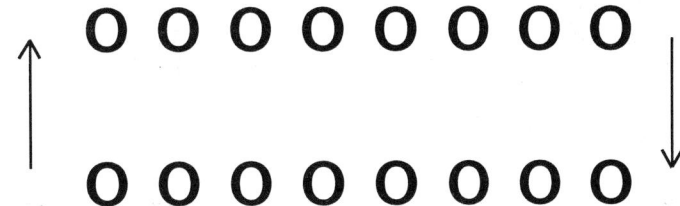

Co-operActivity: Guess the Ending

The story of Sean Landaverde has a happy ending. Sean got the operation to fix his ears, and he looks wonderful! How was it possible? Share your ideas with your group.

13

CHAPTER 2

English Only—At Work

Warm-up

Co-operActivity: Deciding MOST to LEAST

Here is a list of things to look for in a job. Which are important to you? Take 5 minutes to put them in order of most important to least important. Then, check with a partner to see what s/he wrote.

_____ Location	_____ Money
_____ Exciting work	_____ Number of vacation days
_____ Friendly co-workers	_____ Work schedule
_____ Work space	_____ Good medical insurance

Did you and your partner have the same order? Why or why not?

English Only—At Work

Robert Malone is the manager of a small company with 12 employees. Most of the time, the employees speak English. But sometimes during business hours, some of the employees speak to each other in their native language.

Other employees don't like this. They think that not speaking English is impolite and makes them feel unsure about each other.

Robert wants to tell them to speak English only during working hours. He wants to tell them that they can get a bad report or lose their job if they don't.

People think differently about the English-only rule. Some people say it is good because all workers can speak together in the workplace. They say it can stop misunderstandings. Others think that the rule discriminates, or works against people who are more comfortable speaking in their native language.

Talk with your partner or group about Robert Malone's problem. Then, write your opinion in the answer space below.

Answer. _____

_____

_____

_____

_____

Helpful Vocabulary

manager (n.) – person who directs the work of a company, sports team, etc.
employee (n.) – worker
native (adj.) [language] – the first language a person learns
impolite (adj.) – not polite; not nice; bad-mannered
unsure (adj.) – not certain; doubtful
rule (n.) – regulation; order; mandate; law
misunderstanding (n.) – getting the wrong idea from what someone says
discriminate (v.) – treat a person or group differently and unfairly from another

The Talking Edge

Comprehension

Answer these questions. You may look back at the story for the answers.

1. Who is Robert Malone?_____.

2. How many people work in his company?

   a. more than 15   b. less than 10   c. almost 13

3. (**T** - **F**) Robert is unhappy because some employees don't speak English during work hours.

4. What are two different ideas about the English-only rule in the workplace?

   a. _____

   b. _____

Discussion

Answer these questions with a partner or in a group. If you don't have a job, talk about the job of someone in your family.

1. What do you like most about your job?

2. What do you like least about your job?

3. Do people at your job speak only English?

4. Talk about your boss.

5. If you become rich and don't need a job, will you still want to work?

Co-operActivity: Back-to-Back Dictation

You and a partner are sitting back-to-back. One of you is Student A, the other is Student B. You each have half of the story. Take turns with your partner (sentence by sentence) to dictate your parts of the story. Write down what your partner says in the blank spaces. Don't look at your partner's page. **You can say your parts of the story only one time!**

Chapter 2 English Only — At Work

Back-to-Back Dictation

Student A

A man moved away from his town. _____.

He visited all the places _____. He also

visited his old house. _____ when

he moved away. _____ that he had

given to the shoemaker to repair. _____.

The shoemaker was still there! _____.

The shoemaker went to the back of the store. _____

_____ "They'll be ready

on Thursday."

The Talking Edge

Back-to-Back Dictation

Student B

_____ . He returned 20 years later. _____ he often liked to go. _____ . There he found a coat that he forgot to take _____ . Inside the coat, there was a ticket for shoes _____ . He went to the shop. _____ ! He gave the ticket to the shoemaker. _____ _____ . After a minute, the shoemaker returned and said, " _____ ."

Now check your story with your partner to see if you wrote down everything correctly. Do you think this story is funny?

Co-operActivity: Job Role-play

Choose one of the following job ideas. Then, with your group, write a dialog (about 10 -12 lines) to present to the class.

1. You have a chance for a very good job in another state. You will make two times more money than you make now. You have a teenage daughter in high school and a son in junior high school. They both have many friends in your neighborhood. Will you take the new job and move your family? Have a discussion with your family about what to do.

2. Your co-worker, Kay, works very hard. When she comes to the job, she goes to work without saying hello to anyone. She doesn't have an angry face, but she doesn't talk very much during the work day. She often eats lunch by herself. You don't know why she doesn't talk to people. Maybe she is shy, unfriendly, or has a problem. Try to make a conversation with her.

What Does Your T-shirt Say?

Draw a picture of a T-shirt. Write a short expression about "work" on it.

CHAPTER 3

For Love and Money

Warm-up

Co-operActivity: Who Got Audrey's Money?

- Audrey Jean Knauer planned to leave all her money to her family when she died. That is what she wrote in her will in 1977. But, in 1995, Audrey changed her will.

The sentences above begin the story about Audrey Jean Knauer. With your partner or group, try to imagine who got Audrey's money.

For Love and Money

Audrey Jean Knauer planned to leave all her money to her family when she died. That is what she wrote in her will in 1977. But, in 1995, Audrey changed her will. On the top of a shopping list, Audrey wrote that she wanted all her money to go to her favorite actor, Charles Bronson, whom she had never met. She also wrote that if Mr. Bronson did not want the money, it should go to the Louisville Free Public Library. Audrey often went to read about the actor there. She died in 1996 at the age of 55, and Charles Bronson got $300,000.

Her sister, Nancy, says that Audrey was "crazy" when she wrote her will on the top of the shopping list. She says Audrey's first will, which Nancy helped to write in 1977, is the only correct will. That will was signed and witnessed. Now, Nancy wants Charles Bronson to return the $300,000.

Helpful Vocabulary

leave to (v.) – give after death in a will

will (n.) – an official paper that tells where you want your money and things to go after you die

witness (v.) – watch someone sign an official paper, then sign it to show you were present

charity (n.) – organization that gives money or help to people who need it

Comprehension

Answer these questions. You may look back at the story for the answers.

1. What did Audrey Jean Knauer want to do with her money in 1977?

   _____.

2. What paper did Audrey use when she changed her will?

   _____.

The Talking Edge

3. Who was Audrey's favorite actor?

   _____.

4. Audrey said that if Charles Bronson didn't want the money, it should go
   a. to a public library
   b. to her sister
   c. to poor children

5. How old was Audrey when she died? _____.

6. Who was Nancy? _____.

7. What did Nancy say about Audrey when she learned that Charles Bronson got all of Audrey's money?

   _____.

8. (**T** - **F**) Nancy helped her sister write her will in 1977.

9. (**T** - **F**) Nancy helped her sister write her will in 1995.

Discussion

Talk about these questions in a small group.

1. What should Charles Bronson do with the money?

	Yes /No	Why?
a. Keep the money for himself.	_____	_____
b. Give the money to the Louisville library.	_____	_____
c. Give the money to Audrey's family.	_____	_____
d. Give the money to a charity of his choice.	_____	_____

2. Who's your favorite actor? Tell about one of his/her films.

3. Have you ever met a famous movie actor?

Co-operActivity: Guess Who? A Role-play Interview

You and your partner choose one famous actor. One of you will be a news reporter, the other will be the actor. Prepare a television interview between you to present to the class. Be creative! There are many interesting questions to ask. Don't be too clear about who your actor is. Let the class try to guess the actor.

Co-operActivity: Memory Cloze

Without looking back at the story, fill in the blanks for the following two paragraphs. Work with a partner.

Audrey Jean Knauer planned to _____ all her money to her family _____ she died. That is what she wrote _____ her will in 1977. But, in 1995, Audrey changed her will. On the _____ of a shopping list, Audrey wrote that she wanted _____ her money to go to her _____ actor, Charles Bronson whom she had _____ met.

Now check your answers with the first paragraph of the story.

The Talking Edge

Co-operActivity: The Same Face

Sit face-to-face with a partner. Each of you has a blank sheet of paper. Fold it in half, so it looks like a greeting card. You are only going to use the back of the "card" to draw a picture of your favorite relative. **Don't let your partner see your drawing!**

When you finish, turn your card over to the front, and pass it to your partner. Then, describe your relative, so that your partner may draw that person's picture. Give many details in your description. Next, your partner will do the same, and describe his/her relative to you.

Finally, you will exchange papers. Did you do a good job describing your favorite relative?

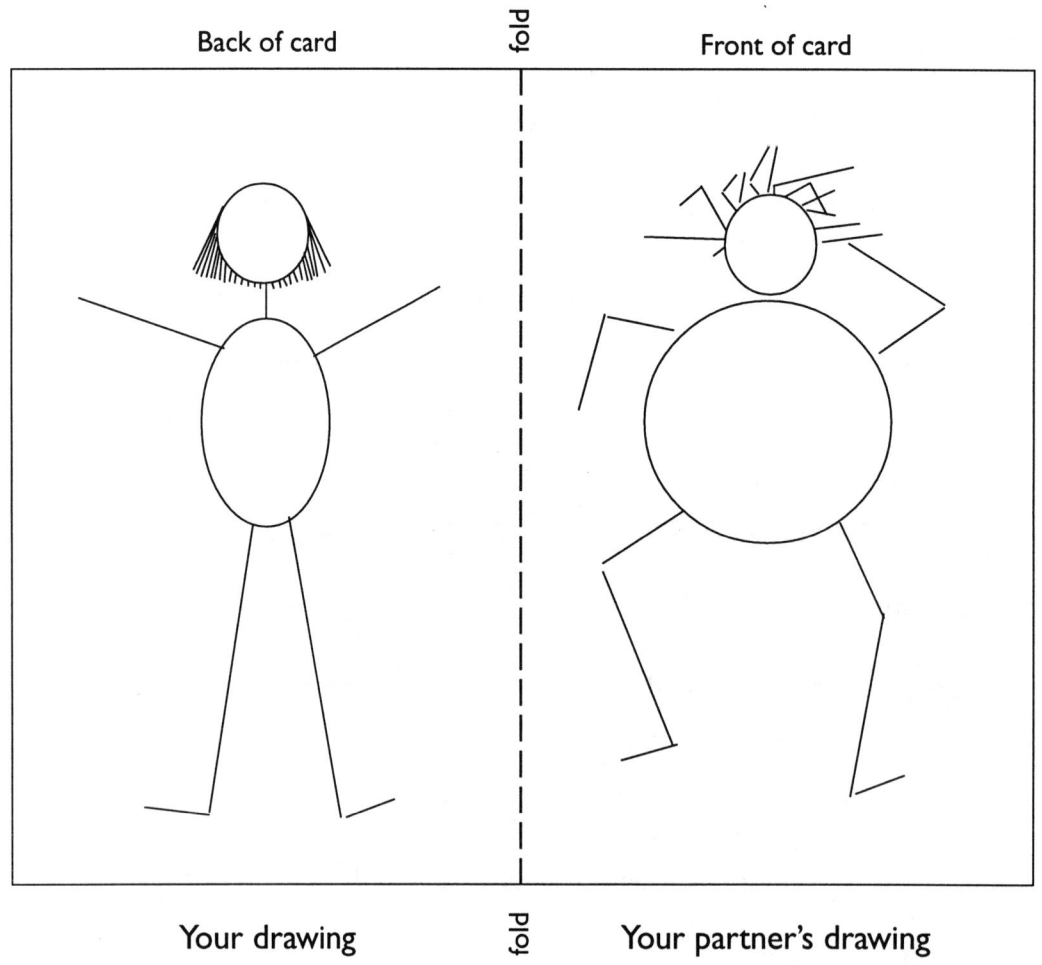

Chapter 3   For Love and Money

Quick-Write

A Quick-Write is a chance to write without stopping to make corrections.

Write a letter to Nancy, Audrey Knauer's sister. Tell her how you feel about Audrey's money.

You have three minutes to write. Go!

CHAPTER 4
Tradition in a New Country

Warm-up
Co-operActivity: Animal Facts Jeopardy

Your teacher will divide the class into two or more teams to play a game of Jeopardy. There are ten Animal Fact questions in the game. Easy questions get 1–3 points. Medium questions get 4-6 points. Difficult questions get 7–10 points.

Choose which team will go first. Then, choose a number below and circle it. Then, listen to the question from your teacher.

Example: "We'll take Animal Facts for 6 points." Then, listen to the question. If your team answers correctly, you get 6 points. If your team doesn't answer correctly, the question goes to the next team.

| 1 | 2 | 3 | 4 | 5 | 6 | 7 | 8 | 9 | 10 |

Tradition in a New Country

Do you want roast chicken for dinner? Do you want to buy the chicken fresh at the live-animal market where someone will kill it for you? Do you want to take the chicken home and kill it yourself? A live-animal market sells fresh chickens, turtles, frogs and fish for food mainly to Asian people. At present, there are 12 of these stores in San Francisco's Chinatown. More and more Asian people are coming to live in the United States, so many new live-animal markets are opening around the country.

Su Chung thinks that fresh chickens taste better and are very healthful. She wants to see the chicken before she buys it. She visits her favorite live-animal store in San Francisco about twice a month. When a chicken is noisy and moves around a lot, she buys that one. Su takes it home and she and her family enjoy the chicken for dinner that evening.

Most of the live-animal markets in Chinatown opened in the late 1800s when many Chinese people moved there. "It is our tradition to buy food this way," said Wei Chen. Her family has lived in Chinatown for nearly 100 years.

But members of an animal rights group in California do not like the live-animal markets in Chinatown. They think that the markets do not take care of the animals very well. They say that chickens, ducks, turtles and other animals are packed into very small wooden boxes. Animals often do not have enough food or water. The animal rights group wants to stop the sale of live animals.

Rose Pak of San Francisco thinks differently. "They do not understand our culture." she told reporters. "These animals are not pets, and these shops are not pet stores. The markets are selling these animals for food."

The Talking Edge

Helpful Vocabulary

roast chicken (n.) – chicken cooked in the oven or over a fire

live (adj.) – living, not dead

noisy (adj.) – making a lot of sounds

tradition (n.) – belief/custom/way of doing something that has existed a long time

animal rights group (n.) – a group that works to make sure that animals are treated well

culture (n.) – the art, beliefs, lifestyle, ideas of a society or group

Comprehension

Answer these questions. You may look back at the story for the answers.

1. What is a live-animal market? _____.

2. In our story, where in California is Chinatown? _____.

3. The number of live-animal markets is getting larger in the United States because _____.

4. How often does Su Chung go to the live-animal market?
    a. two times a month
    b. every two months
    c. every other month

5. Su Chung thinks that fresh chickens _____.

6. "The late 1800s" means

    a. 1800–1824   b. 1825–1849   c. 1850–1874   d. 1875–1899

7. Write two examples that the animal rights group gives for the bad treatment of animals in live-animal markets.

    a._____.

    b._____.

8. Rose Pak says, "The live-animal markets are not _____ stores."

Discussion

Answer this question with a partner or in a group.
How do you feel about people who have different traditions from yours? What are the good things and bad things that can happen when people with different traditions live together? Share your own stories with your group.

Quick-Write

A quick-write is a chance to write without stopping to make corrections.
Imagine you are one of the following people. Write your ideas below.

1. You own a live-animal store in Chinatown. Your family lives from the money you earn at the store.

2. You are president of an animal rights group in San Francisco. You want to stop bad treatment of the animals in Chinatown's live-animal markets.

3. You work in the city. A newspaper reporter asks you what you think about the live-animal markets of Chinatown.

You have 3 minutes to write. Go!

Chapter 4   Tradition in a New Country

Co-operActivity: The $25,000 Vocabulary Game

Make teams of 8 students or less. See the box below for the classroom set up. Sit face-to-face with a partner on your team. One of you can see the board and the other can't. On the board, the teacher writes five vocabulary words taken from the **chapter**. The student who sees the words explains each one to the partner (without using the word or any part of it) to make the partner say the word.

Example: *"Shopkeeper."*
The student facing the board says, *"This is a person who works in the store. This person helps the people who come into the store."*

Partners who finish early may help other teammates. The team to finish all five words first gets a point. Partners change places for the next five words. Now, the other student sees the words. Continue in this way until one team gets five points. That team is the winner!

```
Board   [_____]

Team A    A  A  A  A
          A  A  A  A

Team B    B  B  B  B
          B  B  B  B
```

Your team name: [_____]

CHAPTER 5

Cases of Coffee and Candy

Warm-up

Co-operActivity: Send the Messenger!

Your teacher will place a copy of the story's first paragraph outside the classroom door. Choose partners. One of you is a messenger, the other is a scribe (writer). You and your partner must help each other write down the paragraph. The messenger visits the paragraph as many times as necessary. S/he returns to tell the whole paragraph, a little at a time, to the scribe. The scribe writes what the messenger says. To win, you and your partner must have the paragraph written perfectly.

Cases of Coffee and Candy

You are going to read about two people who had accidents and went to court to get money through a lawsuit. Do you think these are important cases?

The Coffee

Stella Liebeck of Albuquerque, New Mexico ordered a cup of coffee at the drivethrough window of McDonald's one day in February, 1992. This 79-year-old woman got the coffee in a Styrofoam cup. She opened the lid to put in cream and sugar, and the coffee spilled into her lap. Her car was not moving. She was wearing sweatpants, but the coffee burned her skin.

Stella's burns were so bad that she was in the hospital for eight days. The doctors had to graft new skin to replace her burned skin. Stella asked McDonald's for $20,000 because the coffee was too hot. McDonald's told Stella they didn't want to pay. She sued McDonald's to get the money.

The Candy

Andrew Daniels of Ohio bought a small bag of M&M peanut candy from a store one day in December, 1996. He bit down too hard on one piece expecting to taste a peanut. He was surprised. There was no peanut inside. He bit through the chocolate and through his lip! He went to the hospital. Now he is suing the store and the M&M candy maker for $500,000. Andrew Daniels says the candy company and the store didn't check the product for defects before selling it.

A lawsuit is a problem or complaint that someone brings to a court to get money. Some unnecessary, unimportant lawsuits are called "frivolous lawsuits." They are very expensive to fight. Sometimes small companies have to close down, and workers lose their jobs. Is Stella Liebeck's case a frivolous lawsuit? Is Andrew Daniels' case a frivolous lawsuit?

The Talking Edge

Helpful Vocabulary

Styrofoam cup (n.) – heavy plastic cup used to hold hot drinks
spill (v.) – pour out accidentally
sue (v.) – ask for money from someone through a court of law
graft (v.) – take a healthy piece of skin from one part of the body and use it to medically replace damaged skin
expect (v.) – to think that something will happen
defect (n.) – mistake; imperfection

Comprehension

Answer these questions. You may look back at the story for the answers.

1. Stella Liebeck is a _____ woman.

    a. 79 years old   b. 79-year-old   c. 79-year-olds

2. (**T** - **F**) Stella was inside McDonald's restaurant when she ordered a cup of coffee.

3. When did the coffee spill on her lap?
   _____.

4. Did the coffee burn Stella's skin? Yes/No.

5. What did the doctors do for Stella when she was in the hospital?
   _____.

6. Did McDonald's want to pay Stella $20,000? **Yes**/**No**.

7. Where did Andrew Daniels buy his M&M candy?
   _____.

8. When Andrew bit into his candy, he was surprised to find that
   _____.

34

9. Andrew bit into the candy _____ hard.

    a. to   b. too   c. two

10. Andrew thinks he should get the $500,000 because

    a. he bit down hard on the candy.

    b. the businesses didn't check the candy before they sold it.

    c. he was surprised that the candy had no peanut.

Co-operActivity: In Your Own Words

Retell the McDonald's coffee story with a partner. Use the following words to help you to make sentences. Student A starts with the first two words on the A list; Student B says the next sentence using the first two words on the B list. Continue this way until you finish the story.

Student A List

1. Stella, coffee
2. cream and sugar
3. burned
4. skin grafting
5. $20,000

Student B List

1. drivethrough, Styrofoam cup
2. spilled, sweatpants
3. hospital
4. sue, too hot
5. no!

Now, retell the M&M peanut candy story in the same way.

Student A List

1. bag, peanut candy
2. too hard
3. $500,000

Student B List

1. bit, surprised
2. lip
3. defects

The Talking Edge

Discussion

Answer these questions with a partner or in a group.

1. Was Stella Liebeck's lawsuit against McDonald's frivolous?
2. Will Stella Liebeck win her court case?
3. Was Andrew Daniels' lawsuit against the M&M candy company frivolous?
4. Will Andrew Daniels win his court case?
5. Do you know anyone who sued someone in court?
6. Have you ever thought of suing someone? Explain.

Co-operActivity: The line-up

Your teacher writes the names of the main characters on the board and chooses one person to stand under each name. Below are some characters in the stories. Students can call out questions to each character.

Examples of characters for the line-up.

Stella Liebeck	**McDonald's Employee**	**Doctor**	**McDonald's Manager**
(one student)	(one student)	(one student)	(one student)

Andrew Daniels	**Candy Store Owner**	**Doctor**	**M&M Company Manager**
(one student)	(one student)	(one student)	(one student)

Chapter 5   Cases of Coffee and Candy

Co-oper Activity: Skit

You and a partner will act out a scene from one of the stories in front of the class. Choose one of the following scenes. Write a dialog. Then, practice it.

At the Drivethrough Window (McDonald's story only)

Eating M&M Candy (M&M story only)

In the Hospital

In Court

CHAPTER 6

America's First People

Warm-up

Co-operActivity: A Picture Says a Thousand Words

Look at the picture above. In pairs or in a group, discuss what you think this chapter's story is about. Share your story with the class. See which group's story is closest to the real story.

Co-operActivity: Guess the Facts

Read these sentences to get the facts of the story. Only **one** sentence is false. Which one is it? Work with a partner. Do other students agree with you? Say why you think your sentence is false.

> a. Two boys found a man near a lake.
>
> b. The man is 9,300 years old.
>
> c. The man is possibly related to some native American Indians.
>
> d. Some people want to bring the man to a resting place.
>
> e. Some people want to look very carefully at the man.
>
> f. The man was sorry that he made problems for people.

Ask your teacher more questions about the story. S/he can only give you "yes" or "no" answers. You may write your questions here.

_____

_____

_____

_____

Co-operActivity: Pair Reading

You will read the story "America's First People" with a partner, paragraph by paragraph. Read the first paragraph to yourself. When you have finished, you and your partner will tell each other what you understood. Then, read the next paragraph, and stop again to discuss it. Continue this way until you have read the whole story.

America's First People

On July 28, 1996, two young college students, Will Thomas and Dave Deacy, found a human skull by the Columbia River near the town of Kennewick, Washington. "A murder!" they thought. They called the police. The police found more pieces of a skeleton in the water. They sent the bones to a scientist. Tests showed that the skeleton, now called the "Kennewick Man," lived about 9,300 years ago. It is one of the oldest skeletons ever found in the United States.

Native Americans, or Indians, believe that the Kennewick Man is an ancestor. In the past, Indian bones and art work went to museums to be shown or studied. Native Americans told the United States government that they did not want this to happen.

In 1990, a new law was made. It gave American Indians the right to make decisions about bones and art work found on their lands. They want the bones of the Kennewick Man to be buried quickly and without examination. His soul cannot find peace until his bones are buried. "Our culture needs to be respected, too," said one Umatilla Indian.

Scientists want to study the Kennewick Man. They need information about life long ago. It can help them learn about today's human diseases like arthritis and diabetes.

Chapter 6 America's First People

Helpful Vocabulary

skull (n.) – head bones

murder (n.) – killing a person illegally

skeleton (n.) – the bones of a body

scientist (n.) – someone who tests and studies information to gain knowledge

Native Americans (n.) – also sometimes called American Indians

right (n.) – something that you are allowed to do or have

disease (n.) – sickness; illness; unhealthy condition

arthritis (n.) – a disease that makes pain and swelling in the joints of the body

diabetes (n.) – a disease caused by too much sugar in the blood

ancestor (n.) – a member of your family who lived in past times

soul (n.) – the spiritual part of man -not the body

bury (v.) – put a dead body into the ground and cover it so it cannot be seen

culture (n.) – the art, beliefs, lifestyle, ideas of a society or group

Comprehension

Answer these questions. You may look back at the story for the answers.

1. Will Thomas and Dave Deacy are _____ students.

2. What did they do after they found the skull?

    a. They called the police.

    b. They saw a scientist.

    c. They tested the bones.

3. Why is the 9,300-year-old skeleton called the "Kennewick Man?"
   _____.

4. What law was made in 1990? _____.

5. Why are the American Indians interested in the Kennewick Man?
   _____.

6. Why are the scientists interested in the Kennewick Man?
   _____.

The Talking Edge

Discussion

Who should get the bones? Answer this question with a partner or in a group. Write some of your ideas in the box below. Think of reasons for and against each side.

WHO SHOULD GET THE BONES?	
Scientists	**Native Americans**

Next, meet with another pair or group of students and share your ideas. Now, complete this final sentence.

I think the _____ should get the bones.

Co-operActivity: The 45-Second Board Game

How much can you say in 45 seconds?

Play this board game with three or four players. Each player has 45 seconds to talk **non-stop** about the topic in the box. One player chooses a box for another player. If a player does not have any ideas for the topic, the other players in the group can help by asking questions. The teacher will shout "Change!" when the 45 seconds have passed.

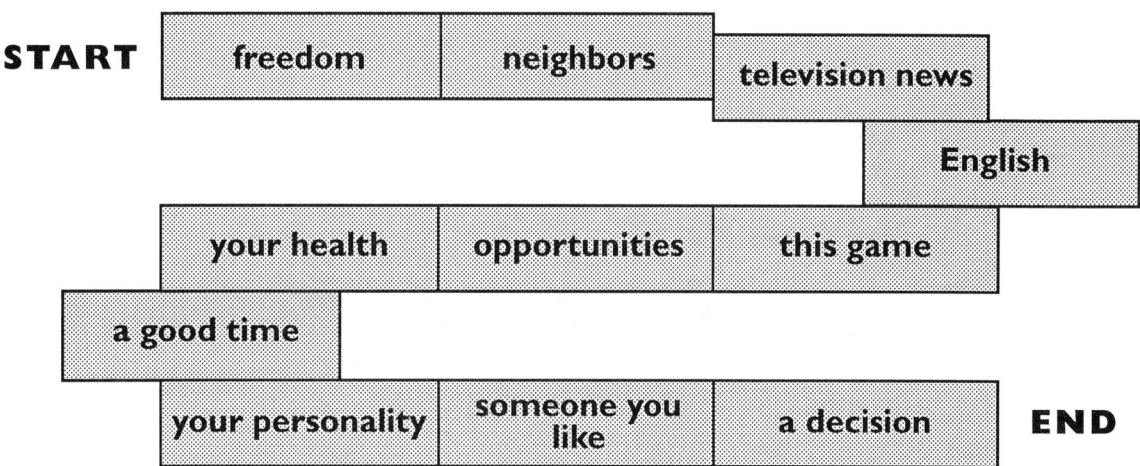

CHAPTER 7

A Good Education

Warm-up

Co-operActivity: Story Relay Race. The class is in teams of five students—one student for each paragraph of the story. One runner from each team goes to the teacher to hear one part of the story. The runner then tells the team what s/he heard. Someone in the group writes the information down. The team changes runners until it has the whole story. All teams play at the same time, and the team that works the fastest wins. Choose a team name before you begin the race. Good luck, and may the best team win!

Team Name:

A Good Education

Mark Hartmann is in the third grade, but he cannot read or write. He makes loud sounds from his chair and waves his hands around his head all the time. He can not listen for more than two minutes at a time. Sometimes, he hits the other children. Sometimes, he also hits his teacher.

Mark Hartmann has autism. His brain cannot organize and manage information clearly. He does not understand the world or the people around him.

The school principal says that the other children lose too much learning time when Mark is in their classroom. She thinks Mark can get a better education at a special program nearby. There, teachers know how to take care of students with autism.

But Mark's parents do not want him to go there. In fact, a law was made in 1988. It says that students with disabilities can be in regular classes. This gives them the same chances for success as everyone else.

The Hartmanns used to live in Chicago. Mark went to regular classes there. Mark had help from some special teachers, and the program was very good for him. "He was part of the school," Mrs. Hartmann told reporters. "He also learned to hold hands with some of the children in his class."

Helpful Vocabulary

loud (adj.)—not quiet

lose time (v.)— not get enough time

disability (n.)— a physical or mental condition that makes it difficult for a person to do things most people are able to do

law (n.)—a rule that people in a country, city or state must obey

The Talking Edge

Comprehension

Answer these questions. You may look back at the story for the answers.

1. Mark is in the third grade, but he cannot _____.

2. How does Mark act in the classroom?

    a. He cannot pay attention very well.

    b. He shouts from his chair.

    c. He hits other children.

    d. All of the above

3. Paragraph 2 explains

    a. autism

    b. Mark's ideas

    c. Mark's school life

4. (**T** - **F**) The school principal wants Mark to stay with his class.

5. (**T** - **F**) Mr. and Mrs. Hartmann want Mark to stay with his class.

6. The 1988 law says that disabled students can have the _____ chances as everyone else.

7. What is good about the "special program" nearby?

    a. The teachers there know more about autism.

    b. It is close to Mark's home.

    c. Mark likes the program.

8. Were Mark's parents happy with Mark's regular school program in Chicago?
Yes/No_____.

Co-operActivity: Counting Nouns

Work with a partner. Circle all the nouns in the story. (Do not include pronouns or proper names.) How many different nouns are there? Put your number in the box. Did you get them all?

Co-operActivity: Facts of the Story

A good story answers certain questions. Work with a partner or a small group. Fill in the blanks below.

Who were the people?	
What happened?	
Place/Time?	
Problem?	

Discussion

Answer these questions with a partner or in a group.

1. Do you know anyone who is disabled? What is his/her life like?

2. Do you think Mark should stay in his regular class or go to the nearby special program?

CHAPTER 8

A Perfect Copy

Warm-up

Co-operActivity: Introduction Cloze

Work with a partner to fill in the blanks of the first paragraph. You may use more than one word in the blank.

A man and a woman from Texas were looking for a _____

when they found Missy at the _____. She was four

months old and very _____. She had a low, strong

_____. Missy was a perfect _____ for the

two people, and they decided to take her home. Now Missy is 11 years old.

Now compare your answers with another pair of students. When you are finished, check the first paragraph of the story. Do you have the same answers?

A PERFECT COPY

A man and a woman from Texas were looking for a dog when they found Missy at the animal shelter. She was four months old, cute and very lovable. She had a low, strong bark. Missy was a perfect dog for the two people, and they decided to take her home. Now Missy is eleven years old.

The man and woman from Texas are now very rich. They continue to believe that Missy is a perfect dog. So, they decided to give Texas A&M University $2.3 million to clone Missy.

Until now, scientists have cloned mice, cows, goats and sheep, but not dogs. Dr. Mark Westhusin is one of the scientists from the University. He and his group of scientists want to learn more about dog cloning. They think the research can help make better rescue dogs and guide dogs for blind people. The scientists at the University are very happy and hope to make several Missy puppies.

Helpful Vocabulary

animal shelter (n.) – place for keeping lost or unwanted animals

bark (n.) – the loud sound a dog makes

clone (v.) – make an exact copy in a science laboratory

scientist (n.) – someone who studies to test and prove facts

research (n.) – the serious study of a subject to find new facts about it

rescue dog (n.) – a dog that has learned to save someone/something from danger

several (adj.) – a few; some

The Talking Edge

Comprehension

Answer these questions. You may look back at the story for the answers.

1. Where did the man and woman find Missy?

   _____.

2. How old was Missy?

   a. four months old   b. four month old   c. four month olds

3. Put a circle around the **three** adjectives that best describe Missy.

   lovable   slow   perfect   strong   cute   old   tired

4. Why did the man and woman want to clone Missy?

   a. because they were rich

   b. because Missy was perfect

   c. because Dr. Westhusin liked dogs

5. Which animals have already been cloned? _____.

6. Write **two** reasons why Dr. Westhusin wants to clone Missy.

   a. _____.

   b. _____.

7. The scientists at the University are very happy and hope to make

   _____ Missy puppies.

Discussion

Choose two of these questions to answer with your partner or group.

1. Do you like pets? Explain.

2. Talk about an experience (good or bad) that you had with an animal.

3. Do you think it is a good idea to use animals for medical study?

4. Do you think one day scientists will clone humans?

Chapter 8   *A Perfect Copy*

Co-operActivity: Story Mix-up

Work with a partner. You have one minute to put the story in correct order.

Number 1 has been done for you.

_____   The man and woman became rich.

_____   They gave Texas A&M University $2.3 million.

__1__   A man and a woman found Missy the animal shelter.

_____   The scientists hope to make several Missy puppies.

_____   The man and woman still think Missy is a perfect dog.

_____   They hope to make better guide and rescue dogs.

_____   The two people decided to take Missy home.

Co-operActivity: Making Questions

You and a partner can use the sentences from the **Co-operActivity** above to practice questions: who, what, where, when, why and how. Afterward, practice answering the questions.

Example: A man and a woman found Missy at the animal shelter.

Where did the man and woman find Missy?

or

What did the man and woman find at the animal shelter?

CHAPTER 9

No Blood!

Warm-up

Co-operActivity: Story Line

There are 15 sentences in the story that follows. You and your classmates will try to put the story in correct order. Your teacher will give you one sentence to memorize. Use a dictionary if you need to. Now, tell your sentence to your classmates. This story is also a puzzle. Can you explain?

1. His son was hurt very badly.
2. They had a wonderful time.
3. The surgeon saw the boy and shouted, "My son, my son!"
4. It was raining while they were driving home.
5. The surgeon washed and went into the room.
6. The road was wet and slippery.
7. Someone called for an ambulance.
8. A man and his son had been to a baseball game.
9. The man had to turn quickly to miss hitting the cat.
10. The ambulance rushed the son to a hospital.
11. Suddenly, a cat crossed the road.
12. He was immediately taken to the operating room.
13. The man died.
14. Can you explain?
15. The car crashed into a tree.

The Talking Edge

Co-operActivity: Get the whole story

The class is in two groups. One group waits outside. The teacher tells the first part of the story to the group inside. The students take notes as they listen to the teacher. Then, the first group leaves the classroom to review the story together, share notes and explain vocabulary.

Next, the second group enters the classroom and follows the same plan using the second part of the story.

Now, in pairs, each student meets with a partner from the other group to get the other part of the story. Students may ask each other questions. In the end, each student knows the whole story.

No Blood!

Part 1

On March 7, 1998, a drunk driver, Keith Cook, hit Jane Russell. She was badly hurt. A helicopter took her to the nearest hospital. The doctors told Jane that she needed a blood transfusion because it might save her life. But Jane, a 55-year-old mother of five children, was a member of a religious group. This group does not believe in receiving blood transfusions. So, Jane refused to have a blood transfusion. She died at the hospital a few hours later.

Part 2

Did the drunk driver, Keith Cook, kill Jane Russell? The jury must decide. If they decide that Keith Cook, the 32 year-old auto mechanic, caused Jane's death, he will spend 15 years to life in jail. But if they decide that Jane's religious beliefs caused her death, Keith will go to jail for four to eight years for driving drunk. He went to jail once before, in 1996, for drunk driving.

Chapter 9 No Blood!

Helpful Vocabulary

drunk (adj.) – not able to control your actions after drinking too much alcohol

blood transfusion (n.) – method of putting new blood in a person's body

refuse (v.) – to say or show that you will not do or accept something

might (modal) – may; possibly; maybe

jury (n.) – a group of 12 people who listen to a case in court and then decide which side is right

cause (v.) – make something happen

jail (n.) – a place where a person is kept for doing something against the law

Comprehension

Answer these questions. You may look back at the story for the answers.

1. Who hit Jane Russell? _____.

2. Jane needed a blood transfusion because the doctors thought it might
   _____.

3. Jane is a _____ mother of _____ children.
                   (age)   (number)

4. Jane did not take the blood transfusion because _____
   _____.

5. (**T – F**) A jury must decide what will happen to Keith.

6. Is this the first time Keith was driving drunk?

The Talking Edge

Discussion

Answer these questions with a partner or in a group.

1. Have you ever seen a drunk driver?

2. What do you think about lowering the drinking age from 21 years old to 18 years old?

3. A doctor tries to save lives. Should the doctor have given Jane a blood transfusion, anyway?

4. Did Keith kill Jane Russell, or did she kill herself?

Co-operActivity: Soap Opera

Work together with a small group of students. Your group is going to write a soap opera-type mini-skit (about 10 - 12 lines of dialog) using the information below. If your group is bigger than 4 students, make extra characters.

> *A man is lying in a room on a hospital bed. He has bandages around his head and body. A doctor and nurse are also in the room. A woman is waiting outside the room. She has something in her hand.*

_____

_____

_____

_____

_____

_____

Chapter 9   No Blood!

_____

_____

_____

_____

_____

_____

Co-operActivity: Classroom Feud

The class is in two teams. One student from each team goes to the front of the class. Each one takes a flag or a noisemaker from the teacher. Then, the teacher shouts a vocabulary word from the chapter. The student who can use that word correctly in a sentence first, raises the flag or noisemaker. The student must say the sentence within 30 seconds to receive a point. An incorrect sentence gives the other team a chance to score the point. The first team to score 10 points is the winner. GOOD LUCK!

CHAPTER 10

Who Will Donate?

Warm-up

Co-operActivity: Make a Story

With a partner or in a small group, make up a story using some or all these words:

eye   bank   note   organ   family   sell

Now, tell your story to your class. See how close you are to the real story.

Co-operActivity: Pair Reading

You will read the story "Who Will Donate?" with a partner, paragraph by paragraph. Read the first paragraph to yourself. When you have finished, you and your partner will tell each other what you understood. Then, read the next paragraph, and stop again to discuss it. Continue this way until you have read the whole story.

Who Will Donate?

Richard Baltierra is looking at the photograph of his only son, Richard Jr., who died. "He was a good son. We loved to go fishing together," says Mr. Baltierra. He is very sad about his 17 year-old son, but he is also very angry.

On July 22, 1996, Richard Jr. was found dead. The police took his body from the family home. Mr. Baltierra, an auto-parts manager, remembers that the police asked him if he wanted to donate any of his son's organs. The father said no.

The next day, he received his son's autopsy report. There was a small note on the report -Corneas CGC24791.47. Mr. Baltierra did not understand the note. At the hospital, they explained that they took his son's corneas and sold them to an eye bank in downtown Los Angeles. Mr. Baltierra was very, very angry.

The law says that corneas are not organs and that hospitals may take them without the family's permission. For many years, the Doheny Eye Bank of Los Angeles has taken and sold thousands of corneas, and family members didn't know.

Continued on next page

The Talking Edge

Continued

The eye bank said that it is trying to do something good for people. Two women in New Jersey are able to see now because they received Richard Baltierra's corneas.

The Baltierra family believes that the eye bank buys and sells corneas to make money. The eye bank usually pays the hospital between $215 and $335 for a pair of corneas. Then, it sells them to transplant centers for between $1,700 to $3,400.

The Baltierras say that the hospital made their family feel more pain and sadness about their son's death because they took his corneas. They are suing the hospital and the eye bank for one million dollars.

Helpful Vocabulary

manager (n.) – a person who directs the work of a company, sports team, etc.

donate (v.) – give something useful to a person or organization that needs help

organ (n.) – part of the body that has a particular function as eyes, heart, liver etc.

autopsy (n.) – examination of a dead body to find out the reason of death

cornea (n.) – the strong, transparent covering on the outer part of the eye

permission (n.) – allowing/letting

law (n.) – system of rules that people in a country, city or state must obey

administrator (n.) – manager

transplant (v.) – medically remove an organ from one person's body and place it in another person's body

sue (v.) – ask for money from someone through a court of law

Chapter 10 Who Will Donate?

Comprehension

Answer these questions. You may look back at the story for the answers.

1. How does Mr. Baltierra feel about his son's death? _____
   _____.

2. What did Mr. Baltierra say to the police on July 22, 1996? _____
   _____.

3. How did Mr. Baltierra know that the hospital took his son's corneas?
   a. He saw a note.
   b. He read the autopsy report.
   c. The hospital told him when he called.

4. Which is **not** true?
   a. The hospital does not need the family's permission to take someone's corneas.
   b. The law says that hospitals may take corneas.
   c. Corneas are not organs.
   d. The Doheny Eye Bank started taking corneas last year.

5. Two women in New Jersey were able to _____ after they received Richard Jr.'s corneas.

6. The Baltierra family believes that the true reason the eye bank buys and sells corneas is to _____.

7. For how much money is the Baltierra family suing the hospital and the eye bank? _____.

The Talking Edge

Co-operActivity: Understanding FOR and AGAINST

People have different opinions about donating organs. Some people, like Mr. Baltierra, think that a person should be buried whole. Here are some other people's thoughts about donating organs. With a partner, write which thoughts are "for" organ donation and which are "against."

FOR/AGAINST

_____ 1. My religion doesn't allow organ donations.

_____ 2. Organ donation is a gift of life.

_____ 3. Donating is too painful for the donor's family.

_____ 4. If I am in an accident, and the hospital knows I am an organ donor, the doctors will not try to save my life.

_____ 5. You are never too old to donate an organ.

_____ 6. My body will be all cut up.

_____ 7. Do not depend on organ transplants. They aren't always successful.

Do you agree with any of the thoughts above? Meet with a small group of students to discuss your opinions about the sentences above.

Discussion

Answer these questions with a partner or in a group.

1. Do you want to donate your organs when you die? Why or why not?

2. Do you know any organ donor stories?

3. Imagine you can choose one person to live forever.?

4. Imagine you can live forever. What things will you do?

5. Do you think Mr. Baltierra will win the case against the hospital and the eye bank?

Write down the most interesting thing you heard from your group's discussion.

_____

_____.

Co-operActivity: Do You Know Your Past Tense?

You will do this activity with a partner. Below is a list of the verbs in the story about corneas. If you are Student A, write the past tense forms for the verbs on your list. If you are Student B, write the past tense forms for the verbs on your list. If you are not sure of the past tense form of some verbs, check with other students who have the same list as yours.

When you have finished, you and your partner will take turns testing each other orally. It is more fun to test each other taking turns with each group of five words.

Add 5 more verbs that you know to your list and test your partner.

Example: | go | <u>went</u> |

Student A

	PRESENT tense form	PAST tense form
1.	love	_____
	go	_____
	say	_____
	look	_____
	be	_____
2.	kill	_____
	take	_____
	remember	_____

The Talking Edge

Student A continued

PRESENT tense form	PAST tense form
tell	_____
want	_____
3. donate	_____
come	_____
see	_____
understand	_____
ask	_____
4. _____	_____
_____	_____
_____	_____
_____	_____

Student B

PRESENT tense form	PAST tense form
1. explain	_____
sell	_____
need	_____
know	_____
try	_____
2. believe	_____
help	_____

Student B *continued*

PRESENT tense form	PAST tense form
buy	_____
make	_____
report	_____
3. pay	_____
wait	_____
die	_____
feel	_____
find	_____
4. _____	_____
_____	_____
_____	_____
_____	_____

Co-operActivity: Vocabulary Mini-Bingo

Choose four words from the **Helpful Vocabulary** list. Write one word in each box below. Your teacher is going to read some word definitions from the list. Mark off each word in your box as soon as you hear its definition. The first student to mark off all four words correctly is the winner!

FREE

CHAPTER 11

Scott's Choice

Warm-up

Co-operActivity: What Happens Next?

Work with a partner. Read the story's first paragraph below. Then, look at the picture above. What must Scott decide? Next, tell your idea to another group. Did you have the same idea?

> Scott Rice and his friends will graduate from high school this summer. They are making plans for the future. But, unlike his friends, Scott has a very unusual decision to make about his future.

Scott's Choice

Scott Rice and his friends will graduate from high school this summer. They are making plans for the future. But, unlike his friends, Scott has a very unusual decision to make about his future.

Scott must decide if he wants to play baseball for the Baltimore Orioles, a major league baseball team, or accept a scholarship to study at the University of Arkansas.

Scott is an easy-going senior with a 3.5 grade point average. He is also a very good baseball player. One day he got a phone call from a Baltimore Orioles representative. He wanted Scott to play for the team. Scott could earn up to $1,000,000 as a beginner player.

But the University of Arkansas also wants Scott. The school has a great baseball team. Scott was able to visit the University and liked it very much. The University offered him a full-baseball scholarship and the chance for a degree.

Helpful Vocabulary

choice (n.) – decision

unlike (prep.) – completely different from

easy-going (adj.) – agreeable; doesn't worry or get angry easily

accept (v.) – take something offered

grade point average (n.) – total grades divided by the number of grades

senior (n.) – student in the 4th (last) year of high school or college

earn (v.) – get money by working

offer (v.) – present; want to give

scholarship (n.) – money given to a person to pay for an education

The Talking Edge

Comprehension

Answer these questions. You may look back at the story for the answers.

1. When will Scott graduate from high school? _____

2. What are Scott's choices?

    a. _____.

    b. _____.

3. Scott is in his _____ year of high school.

    a. 1st   b. 2nd   c. 3rd   d. 4th

4. Write three things you know about Scott.

    a. _____.

    b. _____.

    c. _____.

5. One day he got a phone call from _____.

6. (**T - F**) Scott has a chance to earn $1,000,000 playing for the Orioles.

7. (**T - F**) Scott visited the University of Arkansas and didn't like it.

8. Scott's will not have to pay money to go to the University of Arkansas because the school will give him a _____.

Discussion

Answer these questions with a partner or in a group.

1. Tell your group about a big decision you had to make in your life.

2. What do you think Scott will do? Write some of your group's ideas in the box below.

Chapter 11 Scott's Choice

Scott should play for the Orioles	Scott shouldn't play for the Orioles
Scott should go to the University	**Scott shouldn't go to the University**

Co-operActivity: Vocabulary Through Pictures

Look at the **Helpful Vocabulary** list for this chapter. Then, quickly draw a picture that represents one word on the list. Hold your picture, so everyone can see it. Let your classmates guess which word it is.

Co-operActivity: Word Links

Work with a partner or a group. Talk about how each of these words below relates to the word "**education**." There are no right or wrong answers, only opinions. Can you think of other words connected to **education**?

| teacher | books | friends | television | job | college | communication |
| graduation | home | tests | culture | ____? | ____? | ____? |

69

CHAPTER 12

Women Only

Warm-up

With a partner — talk about a teacher you loved.
— talk about a teacher you hated.

Women Only

Mary Daly is a teacher at Boston College. When she began to teach theology there in 1966, the school did not allow women in her program. So, Mary Daly taught men only. In 1970, Boston College began to allow women into all programs at the school.

Soon after, Mary Daly decided to teach women only. She did not to allow men in her class. She said that women learn better when men are not in the classroom. She wrote many books about women in education. She taught only women for 25 years at Boston College. Then, one male student became angry. He said it was unfair that men could not study in her class. The school said that Mary must allow men in her class. She said no. Now, Boston College wants 70-year-old Mary Daly to leave. They want her to retire. Mary says she is not ready to retire.

Helpful Vocabulary

theology (n.) – the study of religion, religious beliefs and God

allow (v.) – permit; let

male (adj./n.) – man or boy (not woman or girl)

unfair (adj.) – not right

retire (v.) – stop working, usually because of old age

Comprehension

Answer these questions. You may look back at the story for the answers.

1. Mary Daly is a _____ at Boston College.

2. (**T** - **F**) In 1966, women could study in Mary Daly's class.

3. What happened in 1970? _____
   _____.

The Talking Edge

4. Mary didn't want men in her classes because she
    a. didn't like men.
    b. believed that women learn better in classes without men.
    c. wanted to make her program more interesting.

5. One male student said it was _____ that men could not study in Mary Daly's class.

6. Does the school want Mary to teach women only classes? Yes / No.

7. (**T** - **F**) Mary is 70 years old and wants to stop working.

Discussion

Answer these questions with a partner or in a group.

1. What kind of school did you go to?
   All boys?, All girls?, Co-educational (boys and girls together)?

2. Do you think that an all-boys school or an all-girls school is a good idea?

3. Do you think these kind of schools are better than co-educational schools?

4. Do you feel that you can speak freely in co-educational classes?

Co-operActivity: Timed Reactions

Read each sentence below. Think about what you can say about each sentence. Work with a partner. Then, tell your partner what you think about each sentence. **You have one minute to say your ideas.** Take turns talking with your partner about each sentence until you finish all the sentences. Begin your opinions with, "Yes, I think so." or "No, I don't think so." Your teacher will time you.

1. Women learn better when men are not in the classroom.

2. Men learn better when women are not in the classroom.

3. The male student in the story was right to be angry.

4. Boston College should allow Mary Daly to teach women only.

5. Mary should leave Boston College.

Co-operActivity: Ask a Teacher

Interview a teacher. You may ask the teacher your own questions, too. Then, bring your answers back to class. Tell your classmates about your interview.

Question	Comments
1. Why did you become a teacher?	
2. What is your best memory of high school?	
3. What is your best memory of college?	
4. Who are your heroes?	
5. What changes do you want to see in education or at your school?	
6. (Your own question)	
7. (Your own question)	
8. (Your own question)	

Answer Key and Notes to the Chapters

CHAPTER 1 — *An Act of Kindness*

Sources: "Necessary Kindness," Los Angeles Times Editorial Section, 9/7/98; "Managed Care On-Line: Surveys," http://www.mcol.com/survy198.htm; "Summary of Legislation: A Proposal for Action," http://www.hmoabuse.com

Comprehension. 1. Sean is unhappy because he does not want to go to school. Sean is unhappy because he feels different from the other children.
2. No, they aren't. They are unkind. 3. Sean has big ears. 4. …the insurance company thinks it is only a beauty correction.

The Ending. Sean's family found a volunteer group that helps the children of families with little money. Dr. Pecther, a California plastic surgeon, agreed to give his time to fix Sean's ears and make them "normal." Sean is enjoying school very much these days.

CHAPTER 2 — *English Only — At Work*

Sources: "Workplace English-Only Rule," Los Angeles Times Business Section, 9/16/98; "Is Your Company's English Only Rule Lawful?" Christine Cesare and Lisa Lerner, http://www.emmetmarvin.com

Comprehension. 1. Robert Malone is the manager of a small company. 2. c 3. T (true) 4. a. It is good because it can stop misunderstandings. b. It discriminates against people who are more comfortable speaking in their native language.

Did You Know That . . . The Civil Rights Act of 1964 says that an employer may not discriminate against a person because of his/her race, color, religion and sex or *national origin*. The (Title VII) law also says that an employer can make an English-only rule for all employees at the company during working hours.

CHAPTER 3 — *For Love and Money*

Sources: "Sharing His Inheritance," Los Angeles Times - Calendar Section, 4/6/99; Hollywood Online, http://hollywood .com:80/news/topstories/04-06-99/html

Comprehension. 1. She wanted to leave all her money to her family. 2. Audrey used the top of a shopping list. 3. Audrey's favorite actor was Charles Bronson.
4. a. 5. Audrey was 55 years old when she died. 6. Nancy was Audrey's sister.
7. Nancy said Audrey was crazy when she wrote her will on the top of a shopping list.
8. True 9. False

The Outcome. The case never went to court. Charles Bronson agreed to pay Audrey's family an amount of money. Bronson offered the library $10,000, but the library didn't take it. They wanted more money by going to court. Now, the library will receive no money. Bronson donated his part to charity.

CHAPTER 4 *Tradition in a New Country*

Sources: "Animal Rights and Cultural Tradition," Brian Buckley Smith, http://www.vegan.com, 4/6/98; "Cultures Clash Over Live Animals Sold in Markets," Curtius, *Los Angeles Times*, 2/98; "San Francisco Needs Your Help," Poultry Press, 10/96, http://arrs.envirolink.org/upc/f96sf_livemarket.html; Childcraft. Volume 5, World Book Inc., c 1991

Animal Facts Jeopardy. Teachers should use the information below to play.

- 10 points – Which animal can walk underwater? A hippopotamus; a salamander; turtle.
- 9 points – What is the difference between a plant and an animal? An animal moves by itself and eats; a plant doesn't.
- 8 points – Name two birds that cannot fly? A penguin, ostrich, kiwi, emu.
- 7 points – What is the biggest animal present or past? The blue whale. The biggest whale ever recorded was 102 feet long. The heaviest weighed 390,000 pounds.
- 6 points – Which animal is the strongest? An ant. It can lift more than 50 times its weight.
- 5 points – Name the fastest land mammal on earth. The cheetah.
- 4 points – Which animal eats 350 pounds of food each day? An elephant.
- 3 points – What is an animal doctor called? A veterinarian.
- 2 points – Which baby animal rides on its mother's back? An opossum; a koala.
- 1 point – Which animal is the tallest? A giraffe.

Comprehension. 1. A live-animal market is a shop that sells fresh chickens, turtles, frogs and fish for food. 2. Chinatown is in San Francisco. 3. …more and more Asian people are coming to live in the United States. 4. a. 5. …taste better and are very healthful. 6. d. 7. a. Some animals are packed into very small wooden boxes with little food or water. b. Fish in tanks do not have very much water. 8. pet

Outcome. The shopkeepers have promised to improve the treatment of live animals sold in Chinatown markets.

CHAPTER 5 *Cases of Coffee and Candy*

Sources: "High Court Ruling Targets Frivolous Suits," Maura Dolan, Los Angeles Times — California and the West, 12/29/98; "Stopping Lawsuit Abuse," http://www.cala.org/cause.html; "Know the Facts: The McDonalds Coffee Case,"

Answer Key and Notes to the Chapters

http://caoc.com/mcdonald.html; "M&M Case Fine Example of Abuse, Group Says," Alison Hagenah, The Daily Reporter, http://www.sddt.com/-columbus/Files3/9612033.html

Comprehension. 1. b. 2. F 3. The coffee spilled on her lap when she opened the lid. 4. Yes 5. They grafted her skin. 6. No 7. He bought the M&Ms at a candy store. 8. …there was no peanut inside. 9. b. 10. b.

Did you know that… Frivolous lawsuits cost each of us about $1,200 a year. Less than half of the money goes to the injured party; the rest goes to lawyers. M&Ms are 30% brown, 20% yellow and red, and 10% orange, green and blue.

Outcome. In the end, Stella won $2.7 million for her pain, suffering and hospital costs. The $2.7 million equals about two days of McDonald's coffee sales. There are now warning labels that appear on coffee cups across the nation. McDonald's reads, "Caution: Contents Hot." Starbucks has, "Careful, the beverage you are about to enjoy is extremely hot." Check your library or the Internet for any new information about the M&M case.

CHAPTER 6 *America's First People*

Sources: "The First Americans," pgs. 50-57, *Newsweek*, 4/26/99; "The Kennewick Controversies," Constitutional Rights Foundation - The Bill of Rights in Action, Vol.14, No. 1, 12/98; "Skeleton Embodies Debate on America's First People," Kim Murphy, Los Angeles Times, 8/16/97; "A Battle Over Bones," Andrew L. Slayman, Archaeology - Special Report, Vol. 50, No.1, http://www.he.net/~archaeol, 1/97

Guess the facts. f is false.

Comprehension. 1. young college 2. a. 3. The skeleton was found near the town of Kennewick, Washington. 4. A law was signed that gave Native Americans more decision power over their bones and artwork found on government or Indian lands. 5. They want to put his soul to rest. 6. They want to know more about life long ago.

The outcome. In February, 1999, five scientists received the bones. They will decide if the Kennewick Man is an ancestor of the American Indian. If he is, they will return the bones to American Indian tribes for burial.

CHAPTER 7 *A Good Education*

Sources: "Odd Child Out," Marjorie Rosen, *People*, pgs. 113-114, 10/17/94; "Kids Together, Inc.," Individuals with Disabilities Education Act, Part A - General Provisions, Section 601, http://www.kidstogether.org/a-601.html

Comprehension. 1. …read or write. 2. d. 3. a. 4. False 5. True 6. Same 7. a. 8. Yes. Mark was part of the school and held hands with some of the children in his class.

Counting Nouns. There are 30 nouns in the story. Grade, sounds, chair, hands, head, time, minutes, children, teacher(s), autism, brain, information, world, people, principal, classroom, education, program, students, parents, fact, law, disabilities, class(es), chances, success, everyone, part, school, reporters.

Facts of the Story.
- Who were the people? Mark Hartmann, Mark's parents, the principal
- What happened? Mark did not do well with the other children in the classroom.
- Place/Time? In the third grade at school.
- Problem? The principal wants Mark to learn in a special program. His parents want him to learn in a regular classroom.

The Outcome. The court agreed with the school principal. It recommended that Mark attend the special program and occasionally visit some regular classes. Mark's parents removed him from his third grade class and from the entire school district. He now attends classes at a school in another district.

CHAPTER 8   *A Perfect Copy*

Sources: "Animals Are One Thing, Humans Quite Another," Patrick Dixon, Commentaries: Perspectives on Cloning, Los Angeles Times, 12/28/98; "Couple Pay $2.3 Million for School to Clone Dog," Dallas Morning News, 8/26/98; "Cloning Special Report," New Scientist Planet Science, *Bioethics Forum,* New Scientist RBI Limited, 1998; "Cloning Dilemma," E. Chmurak, The Columbia Chronicle, 2/4/97

Comprehension. 1. They found Missy at the animal shelter. 2. <u>a.</u> 3. lovable, perfect, cute 4. <u>b.</u> 5. mice, cows, goats and sheep 6. a. He can learn more about dog cloning. b. He thinks the research can help make better rescue and guide dogs. 7. several

Story Mix-up.
- _3_ The man and woman became rich.
- _5_ They gave Texas A&M University $2.3 million.
- _1_ A man and a woman found Missy the animal shelter.
- _7_ The scientists hope to make several Missy puppies.
- _4_ The man and woman still think Missy is a perfect dog.
- _6_ They hope to make better guide and rescue dogs.
- _2_ The two people decided to take Missy home.

Did you know that... Human cloning may be possible. At this time many scientists are working to clone genetic materials of cells and organs, so they may be used for transplants.

The Outcome. Missy was flown to College Station, the home of Texas A&M University, to have tissue samples taken. According to Dr. Westhusin, the process to clone Missy will take approximately two years. Check for new information at the library or on the Internet.

Answer Key and Notes to the Chapters

CHAPTER 9 *No Blood!*

Sources: "Clinton Calls for Stricter Law on Drunken Driving," M. Cimons, Los Angeles Times, 12/27/98, "Jury to Decide if Victim Was Murdered or Let Herself Die," Ann O'Neill and James Rainey, Los Angeles Times, 12/20/98, "How to Recognize a Drunk Driver and What to Do," Michigan State Chapter MADD, http://www.ring.com/nprofit/MADD/maddtips.html

Story.

- 8. A man and his son had been to a baseball game.
- 2. They had a wonderful time.
- 4. It was raining while they were driving home.
- 6. The road was wet and slippery.
- 11. Suddenly, a cat crossed the road.
- 9. The man had to turn quickly to miss hitting the cat.
- 15. The car crashed into a tree.
- 13. The man died.
- 1. His son was hurt very badly.
- 7. Someone called for an ambulance.
- 10. The ambulance rushed the son to a hospital.
- 12. He was immediately taken to the operating room.
- 5. The surgeon washed and went into the room.
- 3. The surgeon saw the boy and shouted, "My son, my son!"
- 14. Can you explain?

Answer to story puzzle. The surgeon was the son's mother.

Comprehension. 1. Keith Cook, a drunk driver, hit Jane Russell. 2. …save her life. 3. 55-year-old, five 4. …the religious group she belongs to does not believe in receiving blood transfusions. 5. True 6. No. Keith was in jail once before in 1996 for driving drunk.

Did you know that… Drunk drivers cause almost half of all highway deaths.

The outcome. On December 18, 1998, the court decided that Keith Cook helped cause Jane Russell's death but was not guilty of murder. In addition Keith was also found guilty of driving drunk and injuring Russell's daughter, also in the accident. Keith could get up to 15 years to life in jail.

CHAPTER 10 *Who Will Donate?*

Sources: "Reforms on Cornea Harvesting Ok'd," Los Angeles Times, 10/1/98; "Corneas Taken From Body Against Wishes of Kin, Lawyer Says," O'Neill, Los Angeles Times, 5/20/98; "Teen's Parents Tell of Grief in Suit Over Cornea Harvest," O'Neill, Los Angeles Times, 5/13/98; "Top Ten Misconceptions About Organ Donation," http://lserver.aea14.k12.ia.us/dlamasters/Top.Ten.myths.html; "Many

The Talking Edge

Families Say No to Organ Donation," American Liver Foundation, http://sadieo.ucaf.edu/ALFfinal/prognoorgan.html; United Network for Organ Sharing Home Page, http://www.unos.org

Comprehension. 1. Mr. Baltierra is very sad, but he is also very angry. 2. Mr. Baltierra said that he did not want to donate any of his son's organs. 3. a. 4. d. 5. see 6. …make money 7. The family is suing the hospital and the eye bank for $1,000,000.

Did you know that… More than 43,000 Americans are waiting for organ transplants. About nine people die every day while waiting for an organ transplant. Every 16 minutes a new name is added to the national organ transplant waiting list.

Understanding FOR and AGAINST. Only 2 and 5 are "for," the rest are "against".

Do You Know Your Past Tense? Student A word groups. 1. love-loved, go-went, say-said, look-looked, be-was/were 2. kill-killed, take-took, remember-remembered, tell-told, want-wanted 3. donate-donated, come-came, see-saw, understand-understood, ask-asked Student B word groups. 1. Explain-explained, sell-sold, need-needed, know-knew, try-tried 2. believe-believed, help-helped, buy-bought, make-made, report-reported, 3. pay-paid, wait-waited, die-died, feel-felt, find-found

Outcome. Because of the Baltierra lawsuit, the governor of California signed a bill on May 20, 1998. It said that a dead person's corneas can be removed only if relatives agree.

CHAPTER 11 *Scott's Choice*

Sources: "A Royal Dilemma," Milo Peinemann, Our Times; Community News, 6/17/99.

Comprehension. 1. this summer 2. a. play for the Baltimore Orioles b. study at the University of Arkansas 3. d. 4. a. He is easy-going. b. He has a 3.5 grade point average. c. He is a very good baseball player. 5. a Baltimore Orioles representative. 6. True 7. False 8. full-baseball scholarship

Outcome. Scott Rice chose to play for the Baltimore Orioles.

CHAPTER 12 *Women Only*

Sources: "No Boys Allowed," Samantha Miller and Mark Dagostino, People, 6/14/99; "Judge Denies Bid to Stop Retirement b Boston College Professor," Robin Wilson, The Faculty - The Chronicle of Higher Education, 6/4/99.

Comprehension. 1. teacher 2. False 3. Boston College began to allow women in all programs at the school. 4. b. 5. unfair 6. No. 7. False

Outcome. Mary Daly went to court to try to keep her job and continue teaching women-only classes. The court decided that in order to keep her job, Mary would have to allow men in her class. The court's decision is based on a 1972 law that prohibits gender discrimination at schools.